THIS HOUSE

THIS HOUSE

The TRUE STORY of a GIRL and a GHOST

By

AMELIA COTTER

Edited by Michelle Jacksier

Black Oak
MEDIA

This House: The True Story of a Girl and a Ghost

First Edition published by the Author in 2010
Second Edition published by Black Oak Media, Inc. in 2011

First Printing Summer 2011

ISBN-10: 0-9790401-8-3
ISBN-13: 978-0-9790401-8-4

Published by Black Oak Media

1. Ghosts—Maryland. 2. Haunted houses—Maryland. 3.
Paranormal research. 4. Maryland—History and folklore. 5.
Young adult romance.

To order copies of this book contact:

Black Oak Media, Inc.
Rockford, Illinois
www.blackoakmedia.org
orders@blackoakmedia.org

Printed in the United States of America.

Praise for *This House: The True Story of a Girl and a Ghost*

"This is exactly the kind of book that, as a young woman, fueled what eventually became in me a full-time career in professional ghost hunting. Ms. Cotter's evocative writing deliciously transported me to my earliest days of searching, when I first found respite—as she does—in our most unusual, shared profession. With each word, I left my busy adult life and career, with all its responsibilities and certainty, and was a girl again, searching for answers within and without, finding solace in the mysteries of the past and their place in our lives. A wonderfully engaging book which also sheds light on the complex impulses that make the paranormal so irresistible. Ghosts speak to us in so many ways. The author is a master listener."

—Ursula Bielski, author of the Chicago Haunts series and founder of Chicago Hauntings

From Amazon reviews:

"This House was one of the best books I have read in a long time. After a few pages I found myself drawn into the story and had a difficult time putting this book down."

"Not only was it a great ghost story but it also brought me back to my childhood. In a way, it's a coming of age story, teen romance, and ghost story all rolled into one."

"This book is very well written and thrilling—it will submerge you in a world shrouded in legends."

Black Oak Media titles by Amelia Cotter:

This House: The True Story of a Girl and a Ghost

Maryland Ghosts: Paranormal Encounters in the Free State

Other titles by Amelia Cotter:

Breakfast with Bigfoot (ages 3-6), Barclay Bryan Press

For My Parents

Contents

Acknowledgments

First I would like to extend a very special thank you to Michael Kleen and Black Oak Media for publishing this updated edition. I am so thrilled that *This House* has found a good home. Also, a very warm thanks goes to my editor, Michelle Jacksier, and Ursula Bielski. I would also like to thank my friends and family for their support, especially Gretchen Hendrick, Carlos Olvera, Sarah Gowen, Daniela Daus, and Mom & Dad. Thanks as well to all the special people and places in Maryland that have loaned their names and inspiration to this book. And finally, thank you to all the awesome readers and fans.

Foreword

I first met Amelia in the spring of 2010 in a claustrophobic café called Charmers on Chicago's north side at a Chicago Ghost Hunters Meetup. I had been asked to come and speak about the *Legends and Lore of Illinois*, a monthly newsletter concerning some of Illinois' most notorious locations, as well as my most recent books. Amelia immediately struck me as a genuine person, and she was someone who commanded the room with a pleasant, matriarchal flair. Of course, I only found out later that she had survived a battle with cancer, which certainly attests to the strength of her character.

I was delighted to learn that she was also an author, which makes sense in a way because writers, if they stick with their craft, must have a certain dogged tenacity to their character that makes them keep going long after most other people would have given up. Hardly anyone, after all, faces more rejection than writers.

Some of us, tired of receiving rejection letters and convinced our work is worthwhile, turn to the masochistic act of self-publishing. Most of these endeavors inevitably fall flat, but occasionally there is an exception to the rule. Amelia Cotter's *This House* is such an exception. Something about this little book connects with its readers like a tiny, gleaming stone mysteriously jumps out from a jewelry counter. It is a charming coming of age story with a macabre twist, perfect for a time when interest in the paranormal is at an all-time high.

When Amelia said she was looking for a publisher for a second edition of This House, I jumped at the opportunity to add it to my catalog. Black Oak Media has been blessed with a series of talented authors, and I have no doubt that our readers will thoroughly enjoy this book. Let *This House* take you back to a time when the barrier between the real and the imagined was mercurial and all things seemed possible. Who knows, you just may discover something of yourself lurking in these pages.

— Michael Kleen

Black Oak Media

Summer 2011

Introduction

I feel very lucky to be sitting here writing an introduction to the second edition of my beloved first book. The hard work and time spent navigating the ins and outs of self-publishing over the past two years have finally paid off.

I am still thankful that I got to spend six months at home in 2007 and early 2008, writing this book and dreaming of becoming an author, in spite of the less than ideal circumstances of also being in treatment for Hodgkin's lymphoma. Oddly, it was the perfect time and place to just sit down and write. Having only one thing to focus on—getting better—created the ideal environment for literary inspiration and a bit of nostalgia to come together. The writing of this book helped me get through one of the most difficult and painful times a person can experience, and it helped me to reconnect with my childhood in a positive and romantic way.

Thus, my intentions with telling the world this ghost story have less to do with idealizing a strange and potentially dangerous paranormal "relationship" than with celebrating the hope, fear and magic of childhood and growing up.

The story is told through the eyes of a character, Nora, who is 15 and a bit older than I was at the time these events occurred. I was eleven when I first set foot in "Walter's house" and twelve by the time it was torn down. The majority of events in this book did happen, and they're told like a story because memories *are* like stories— they're fluid, fantastic, melodramatic, overblown, and they exaggerate the small details while completely forgetting about some of the big ones.

I also chose Nora's character and age to give the story an artistic twist, as well as make it more palatable for a wider audience. Not all people can relate to—or are amused by—the idea of a little girl exploring an abandoned haunted house alone. It's amazing what just a few years can do.

Other names have been changed as well. My original journal entries included in the last chapter provide the final momentum and clarification for understanding the scope and reality behind what really happened.

Ultimately, *This House* is just a small memorial to two parallel times in my life of great mystery and adventure. My lifetime of experiences with the paranormal, including the ones in this book, as well as the rollercoaster of having and recovering from cancer, continue to teach me that there is so much beauty and wonder in the world, and most of it is not as far beyond our reach as we think.

Also, this is not just my story. It belongs to everyone who enjoys stepping out of their comfort zone, taking chances, and exploring the unknown. It's also the story of the book's star ghost, "Walter," whose otherworldly inspiration has touched the lives of many people, and even created a writing career. I'm sure that if he could tell the living one thing, he would say that the simplest things in life can be treasures, and there is no physical or metaphysical limitation on how much we can love—or what we can achieve, in this life and beyond.

I hope the story within these pages will frighten, inspire, and engage the child, the romantic, and of course, the ghost story geek in you, as it has in me.

— Amelia Cotter,
July 19, 2011

This House

By day, it was empty. By night, it was haunted.
The house was old and caving in.
It was ancient, and it smelled awful, and it was musty.
It was hidden behind large, forbidding trees.
It was a careless house.
The walls were coming down.
One touch could send it toppling to the ground.
Shattered glass and rusted nails were its greatest
qualities.
It was gray, and rotting, and ugly.
It was my favorite place in the world.

— Amelia Cotter,
January 18, 1998

One: I Remember

I was at work reading a book, it was the middle of the day on a Wednesday, and there were no visitors in the museum. Jen and I were sitting in the main welcome room, which used to be the dining room of the nineteenth century mansion, now a Civil War field hospital museum. The summer air was still, even at the top of the hill overlooking the crisp brown fields of corn that were barely alive in the July heat.

I was in my own little world, when out of nowhere I heard the doorknob jostling in the next room—the kitchen. I instinctively gasped and turned in my seat, trying to look out the window to see if someone was trying to get in from that side of the house. It was not an entrance. Jen had been staring into space a while and also looked around suddenly. "Hey, did you hear that?" she asked dreamily at first, then got up quickly.

I had a direct view to that part of the outside leading up to the kitchen. There was no one in sight. "There's nobody out there," I said.

"I didn't hear anything from outside, I heard a noise in here," she said nervously, going into the kitchen. The kitchen was separated from us by an original brown wooden door. I could hear her muffled voice in the other room. "Huh, I swear I heard the light switch go up."

I came down off my stool and around the counter, heading for the kitchen. "Well I heard someone trying to open the door."

I entered the kitchen. The light was off. An even taller and heavier brown door stood across the room, leading to the outside and a little path that wound around the house. That's where the sound had come from.

The door was closed. Jen was inspecting it. She looked down at the latch. "No way, check it out, Nora," she said, trying to turn the knob. I stalked over there slowly, sluggish from the heat, and could feel my eyes widening.

I wasn't scared, just amazed. The latch had been lifted all the way up and was resting on top of the metal part that barred the door from opening inward. It took all the strength in my forearms to push it off the metal part and back into place. Someone with an excellent grip had definitely turned that knob, either from the outside or the inside.

"That's crazy," I said softly. The house was known for its ghosts, but I had been there so many times—sometimes all alone and in all types of weather—and had never witnessed a single paranormal event that couldn't be explained by my own imagination. "I guess maybe we do have a visitor."

"Old Mrs. Richardson just wants us to know she's here, I guess," said Jen, shaking her head. "Wow. I've got the chills now." She turned and went back into the other room.

"You know," I started, following her, "it's always the subtle stuff that's the creepiest, isn't it?"

"I guess so. Now, I don't know what would happen if she decided to show up right in front of us in all her glory. That would probably kill me. But this kind of thing is freaky, too. Like, why would you decide to jiggle the doorknob of all things?" She brushed off her butt and sat down on the staircase.

"Yeah, I agree. It's just unsettling. Have you ever actually seen a ghost?" I asked, taking my place on the stool behind the counter again.

"Well," she started with a heavy sigh, "yes I have. This happened when I was a kid, and I was about six years old, so I do take it with a grain of salt.

"And this was it. Since then I have never had anything spooky happen and I am not really into ghost stuff either. There could be ghosts all around me all the time and I would have no clue. I'm just not sensitive like that. But anyway..."

I wiggled in my seat and got ready. Today might be an interesting day after all. "Tell me, I love a good ghost story."

"Oh, I know you do. Okay. So this happened this one time, and it was on Halloween...I know, I know. I was about six years old, and I was on the street by myself. It was getting dark, and I don't remember why I was alone, but I was by myself for just a few minutes, maybe ahead of or behind the others in my group. Who knows?

"Well, I had this compelling feeling like I should look up and across the street. It was dusk and so the sky was, like, light at the bottom but really dark at the top, and I saw this man walking in my direction. But he wasn't solid, he was more of an outline, and it was like a greenish glowing outline."

I started snickering and she paused.

"What?" she asked, grinning widely. "I'm just telling you what happened! He was green, deal with it. And I wasn't scared, but like, more puzzled and interested, and then he just faded away. I didn't get a good look at his features, nothing. He was just gone."

She waited, thinking. "But I can still see the whole thing really clearly in my mind."

I thought about it. "That is pretty cool, I guess. I mean the glowing part is kind of strange, kind of cheesy, but I have heard stories like that. And it for sure, one hundred percent was not a dream?"

"No, no. My Mom still remembers me telling her all about it. But I have no recollection of what happened right before or right after. It was like I was in this weird time warp for a second, and then it all went back to normal. My Mom told me I was really confused for a few minutes and then I was totally fine again."

I nodded, impressed.

"What about you?" she asked me. "Did you ever see a real ghost?"

I thought briefly, flipping through the pages and pages of odd noises, bad dreams, mysterious toilet flushes, and bumps in the night that had terrorized me when I was a child. And then I remembered something so intimate and strange that I hadn't told anyone about in years.

"You know," I said, laughing uncomfortably and nodding, "I *have* seen a ghost. It's not something I think a whole lot about anymore. But you know, I had this whole saga in my life surrounding this house when I was younger. It was abandoned and supposedly haunted. Well, I mean, it *was* haunted. I actually got to meet the ghost."

She raised her eyebrows, intrigued.

But suddenly I was looking down at my shoes. All of these old emotions came rushing back. It wasn't that I had dared to forget, I just hadn't stopped to remember in a *very* long time.

How strange that on this day—not long after I had graduated from college and was spending the summer thinking about the meaning of life and all sorts of wonderful deep things—it came creeping up from the past to find a niche to fill again.

So I told Jen the whole story. A warm and welcoming breeze blew through the room, transporting us back to that late summer when I had no idea I was about to fall in love with a ghost...

Two: It Begins

I was fifteen, still developing in a number of ways, and not the prettiest girl in those days. I was too tall for my age, my hair was bone straight, and my legs were long but I was athletic and my hips were just too wide for the guys to take any interest in me. Yet. It was a brutal combination for a girl in the tenth grade. But I was really smart and funny, so most people kind of liked me.

Still, I had a little loneliness issue, like most people my age. I longed for what lie beyond the suburbs. For me, that mystery was exemplified by the supernatural.

I fancied myself the great ghost hunter, but with no driver's license and no money, I barely had the means to do any real exploring. The Ouija board got old and boring at parties very quickly, and I would always listen to my friends tell riveting tales of their haunted houses, all the while wishing I had such excitement in my life.

All of this changed very quickly when Dad came home from his new job one day, and started casually telling me and Mom about the haunted house on the property. Dad worked at a restaurant out in horse country in Baltimore County. The restaurant sat on My Lady's Manor, a 10,000 acre plot of land that had been owned by the third Lord Baltimore, Charles Calvert, which he had built for his wife in 1713. The restaurant itself had formerly been used as a horse stable for the inn across the street, and then as a tavern sometime in the eighteenth or nineteenth century, until it was converted into a restaurant in the 1980s.

The property was huge, but in the central area of the restaurant stood about three houses in a row along the road. I imagine they were built later than the original manor and were used by regular tenants until they were abandoned sometime in the 1950s. One of them was newly restored and occupied by a young mother and her son, and one stood abandoned by the road behind a row of trees. The third one was at the very end of the property, on the edge of the road, collapsing and buried under vines and overgrowth.

In addition to the restaurant being haunted by a shadowy man who would sit by the fireplace late at night, the abandoned houses were also rumored to be haunted. The lady who lived in the restored house talked about her son's fire trucks moving around by themselves in his room when no one was there, their sirens blaring.

The other house that wasn't completely dilapidated was supposedly fit for exploring and had been broken into by teenagers and homeless people a lot. There was rumored to be an old bookcase inside with antique books still on the shelves.

People dining out on the terrace of the restaurant reported hearing shouts coming from inside that house at night, and others would see the silhouette of a man in the windows.

As soon as I heard about all this, I knew I had to go there. This would be Nora's golden opportunity. I dreamt of what it might look like there. I gathered up all my ghost hunting equipment—that is, my notebook, flashlight, point and shoot camera, and a tape recorder—and put it in a backpack. All I needed to do was sit and wait for my great ghost hunting career to begin.

Every once in a while, Mom would need to use my parents' only car during the evening, so when Dad worked nights we would have to drop him off and pick him up very late. This was a great time to put on my headphones and enjoy the fresh air of a night drive. As enthusiastic as I was about seeing the place, Mom decided that the next time we drove out there to pick him up, we would snoop around a little while waiting for him—even if it was a school night.

So in the meantime, I probed the old man for more information. Every day I asked him if he had heard any new stories. He usually shrugged and said he had asked around but gotten nothing, but once in a while he had a good one. I wrote everything down in my special notebook until I was able to piece some information together.

I figured out this much: the story of the haunting was pretty complicated. There seemed to be at least two ghosts, one man and one woman, but they all went by one name—"Walter." The explore-worthy abandoned house was also known as "Walter's House."

Legend had it that the name Walter came from an incident that occurred one quiet morning when a cleaner was in the dining room all by himself. He was busy vacuuming the floor when a lady in Victorian-style dress drifted into the room, approached him, and asked him, "Where is Walter?"

She then proceeded to walk through a wall and disappear. Needless to say, the cleaner quit his job that day and was never seen by anyone in the restaurant again.

Well, naturally I was thrilled to hear this story, and hoped I might be lucky enough to meet this lady one day, or at least cross the threshold of the house supposedly belonging to a man named Walter.

On a still and warm night in September, I threw my backpack in the backseat, Mom put our flashlight in the cup holder, and we drove out late to pick Dad up from work. On the way I felt nervous and elated, daydreaming while watching the moon and the dark silhouettes of trees go by. The drive consisted almost entirely of fields and wooded areas, some abandoned barns, and a graveyard. The tone was set.

As we turned onto the road the restaurant was on, Mom told me to look out my window to the right and through the trees to see the house.

Sure enough, as we slowed down to get a good look at it, I glimpsed over the guardrail and through a row of evergreens to the black expanse of a large old house. I could feel my heart thudding in my ears. It was like a giant monster sitting behind a cage at some sideshow, watching us watching it. I had a feeling of horror and elation all at once. We passed it slowly and soon pulled into the parking lot of the restaurant.

We curved around and drove back to the farthest edge of the parking lot where no one else was parked. Our headlights stared straight into the back and the side of Walter's house. It stood slightly apart from the restaurant and its companion house. We couldn't even see the other, more dilapidated, house at the road's edge.

Where there was light and noise and laughter coming from the terrace behind us, there was a sudden and overpowering darkness and seclusion in the house's direction. The house was completely alone.

As I got out of the car and fumbled for the flashlight, I realized how nervous I was and how frightening and ridiculous the thought of actually entering an abandoned house at midnight might be. It was someone's house after all, and once upon a time it had been occupied by peoples' lives and feelings and energies.

I couldn't take my eyes off of it.

It was as if the house was watching us and knew we wanted to come in, like there were a bunch of people gathered at the windows waiting nervously for us to try and break in.

I suddenly didn't want to go in there.

"There's old Walter's House," Mom said casually and slammed the car door. I shuddered. I didn't want anyone to hear us. "Let's go, Nor," she said. I walked up alongside her, turned on the flashlight, and we started towards the house.

"I have an uneasy feeling," I admitted quietly.

"That's 'cause this place is creepy as hell," she responded, holding my wrist for comfort.

"That must be it," I agreed, laughing uncomfortably.

We approached cautiously. The unfortunate thing about flashlights is that they light up everything in front of you very nicely but make what's to the sides of you and at your feet pitch black. You'd think I would have noticed that sometime in my life before this.

As we turned the corner of the porch and came to stand in front of the house, I looked into the old broken windows and was filled with fear. I wasn't scared of any living people, but something else. And I could *feel* that something all around us.

I could smell the old sour odor of rotting wood and water damage. It also dawned on me that this could be very dangerous. Would it not have been wiser to first explore the place in the daytime? We didn't even know if the floors were stable in all places.

I looked all around me. The porch spanned the front of the house and was caving slightly in the middle. There was a second floor with a row of broken windows. Up on the side of the house were two tiny black attic windows, typical of historic houses in Maryland. Those windows were like two black eyes peering down at us.

I couldn't decide if it was the house or someone or *something* in it that was watching us.

The front screen door was hanging on its hinges in the moonlight, but the front door itself stood wide open. Even with my own mother there, I felt alone and terrified. All of my friends were probably at home sleeping, on the phone, or watching TV, and I was standing in front of an empty 200-year-old house with a flashlight and a backpack.

"I don't think—" I started.

"I'll go in first," Mom said, taking the flashlight and hopping up onto the porch. She tripped a little. "Careful. Follow closely behind me."

"Thanks for the tip," I said and fumbled and tripped and pulled myself up onto the deceptively high porch. "Shine the light on me, on me!" I whined nervously as the light went all over the door frame and into the house. I stood right up close behind Mom, and held my breath. As we entered, I felt an immediate sensation of being unwelcome. The musty stench I had smelled before became overwhelming. We did not belong there.

"God, I feel like someone doesn't want us here," Mom whispered.

"Really?" I asked, feeling my eyebrows clench together. "I was just thinking that."

We stepped over the threshold and were immediately greeted by a cluttered staircase going up to the second floor. "The floor seems sturdy," Mom said. "Dad said people come in here all the time, so we should be fine. Just watch your step. Feel first before you walk."

I didn't answer, just nodded. To the left and right were large rooms filled with clutter and trash, and some tables and chairs that looked like the foldable lawn type. I could see a fireplace in each room, which must have been very cozy at one time. No bookshelves yet. And I couldn't make out what was in the back of the house. Everything on the periphery of the flashlight's beam was disturbingly black.

We looked from left to right and decided to go to the right, inching through what was presumably the living room. I gripped the back of my mother's shirt with my fist.

The light from the flashlight shined onto an old-fashioned kitchen stove and sink at the very back of the house, in what seemed to be a more recent addition. There was even a 1950s style sun porch at the far left. There was stuff all over the floor in there and it was clearly too cluttered to enter. It amazed me how long this place must have stood abandoned.

I looked down at my feet and saw that I was stepping on all kinds of old newspapers and magazines. I had just started to take an interest in the place when I looked to my left and saw a gaping black hole in the wall—a doorway.

"Hey, what's this for?" I asked, and took a step towards it. Mom shone the flashlight on it, but it was too late for me to step back. I found myself reading the words "Stairway to Hell" in green spray paint with an arrow pointing down and to the right. My eyes followed the direction of the arrow and I found myself staring at the dirt floor of the basement below.

My feet were inches from the nonexistent staircase. Out of surprise and the feeling of being watched from down there, I jumped back and shouted.

The shouting must have spooked my mother because all of a sudden she started shrieking along with me. There was a moment of almost amusing panic where we both stood still, taking turns shouting, and then we suddenly scrambled for the doorway to get out of the house.

Mom leapt ahead with the flashlight and turned back to light my way. We jumped off the porch and ran back around the side of the house where we had come from.

I was running for my life, like I could feel something was coming after us and was just going to get me for sure. We headed for the car and as I looked back, I swear I thought I saw feet coming through the grass after us.

Well, the time from the Stairway to Hell to the safety of our car must have been all of five to seven seconds. The parking lot was safe territory again and the dim light that emanated from the restaurant felt like "base" in a game of tag. I looked back at the house. It was just sitting there, still, dignified.

It was definitely haunted.

At a loss, we both just started to laugh. "Did I scare you?" I asked, out of breath.

Mom was pale and shaking. "No," she said. "I thought I heard a noise when you were looking down that staircase. And then you screamed, and I assumed you were screaming about what I heard. And so with seeing those words on the wall and the noise, I mean, everything happened so fast. I don't know what to think."

A noise, I wondered. "What kind of noise?"

"Just a creaking."

I looked back at the house again. It was so mysterious. I was terrified but already wanted to go back again. "Maybe we can visit again, in the daytime sometime?" I asked.

"Yeah, let's do that. You're not too scared now, are you?" She laughed.

"No, I think we might have scared ourselves."

We got into the car. She turned it on and we drove around to where we normally picked up Dad. He was waiting there for us.

He opened the door and stuck his head in the car. "Hey kids, did you guys go into...*Walter's House?*" he asked dramatically.

Over the next several days and nights, I couldn't get over what had happened. I thought about it all the time. It might not have lasted long, but it was an adventure. It was the first step in my harrowing career as a ghost hunter. I told everyone who would listen all about it. I told all of my friends at school. I recorded it in my ghost hunting log book—my very first "fieldwork" entry.

I was obsessed with the next time I could go back and see the place in the daytime. The words "Walter's House" already began popping up randomly on my notebooks and binders at school. If I had a free minute to think, ghosts were on my mind, and I inadvertently began to construct my vision of what Walter, or whoever the ghost was, might look like and who he might have been. Not to mention that this place was a veritable goldmine—I had access to it all the time and it was like my own little secret.

My only disappointment was that I hadn't found that old bookshelf Dad talked about yet.

"Maybe it's upstairs," he suggested. I would soon find out.

The weather was getting cooler, but I didn't need a jacket just yet. I liked the feeling of the chilly air on my skin, the way it smelled, and the way the sky deepened to a bright robin's egg blue.

We pulled up to the same spot we had parked in a few nights before, only it was the height of the afternoon. This time Dad also came along and was equally as eager to have a look around. The whole family seemed to be morbidly curious about this strange place.

In the daytime, the house was still as large as I had remembered, only now I could take in all of its intricate details and see how beautiful it truly was. It still looked imposing and the eyes of the attic windows gazed down at me as we approached—still black in spite of being broad daylight. The glass had broken away from the windows long ago, leaving nothing there but space between us and whatever it was that was watching us.

But I was so taken with it that I started snapping photos without hesitation, and was only vaguely aware of being watched.

The wood was more or less a uniform gray color. It was a tired old house with no trace or hint of original paint. It appeared sturdy though, and I had to wonder why no one had ever fixed it up and given it a good paint job. The sides and the back of the house, up to about ten feet or so, were covered by the last vines and greenery of the season. The added-on covered porch in the back was nearly collapsing under the weight of a tree growing straight up through it.

We walked around to the front of the house, where the vegetation was thicker under the shade of the evergreens and other trees near the road. I saw that the porch was actually caving in dangerously, and the floor was slanting in from both sides at a sharp angle. I hadn't noticed that before.

The screen door remained in its lazy leaning position, swinging gently back and forth and creaking ever so slightly.

The house, though it had confident energy, just seemed to slump inward a little. I hopped up onto the porch with my own confidence intact—so far—and went inside.

In the daylight, I still felt uneasy, but much of that foreboding "any second something terrible is going to happen" feeling was gone. There was that familiar odor of old wood and condensation. Once again, I was quickly overcome with the distinct impression that we were not welcome. I looked down at the paper and clutter at my feet. I walked carefully and respectfully, hoping in some weird way that the house and its occupants would notice how delicate I was being.

I walked slowly over to the basement stairwell, my parents trailing behind me and chatting about how cool the house was. I wasn't really listening; I was in my own place. I looked into the stairwell again, which I had previously mistaken for a closet. A shelf held the remains of several empty Mason jars. The words "Stairway to Hell" seemed more like a bad joke now, but when I glanced down into the basement again, that sickening feeling came back.

"Boy, it is scary," Dad confirmed, walking up behind me and looking over my shoulder. "Wow, you girls came in here at night. I don't think I could do that." We walked over to the small kitchen, only getting about a foot or two into the room. As I had seen the other night, there was rubble and siding piled up all around the appliances. The old refrigerator door stood halfway open. I would have liked to see what was inside, but there was no accessing it. There were ancient empty cans of powdered milk on the counter.

I wondered what kinds of snakes and spiders lived underneath all the piles of trash and calendars and broken records that were lying around. I took more pictures. As I looked around, I wondered what would make whoever had lived here move out in such a hurry and just leave everything behind.

"Wanna' try the upstairs?" Dad asked us.

"Yeah," I answered.

"I dunno, it looks like the stairs are pretty treacherous," Mom answered. "I think I'll stay down here."

No come on. You have to come, too," he said.

Dad and I made our way back to the staircase. Mom was already standing there looking up to the second floor. I glanced into the other room. It was a good thing Mom and I hadn't tried taking a left on our previous expedition, because if we had gone in there, we would have fallen right through the floor. About half of it was missing, leaving a gaping black hole in the room. That gave me a very dark, unsettled feeling. I turned quickly and looked up the stairs, snapping a photo. All I could see was more clutter and another open doorway.

Dad started up slowly, feeling his way with his foot outstretched, looking for soft spots in the floor. The stairs creaked dramatically and Dad hesitated, finding his footing. He continued slowly.

Mom reluctantly followed. I didn't like the feeling of being last, or alone downstairs, so I started up after them. The stairs felt soft under my feet.

In spite of my hesitation, there was something compelling me to go up. So I was scared, but I went.

I stepped onto the landing and looked around. To my left and immediate right were two bedrooms, and in front of me there was a bathroom. To the far right there was another bedroom. None of them seemed accessible to me except the room to my immediate right. Rubble and more piles of wood or trash blocked the other doorways, and the floor was rotting or nonexistent in some areas. Except for some tree branches and vines creeping in through the broken vacant windows, the upstairs retained its uniform grayness. And yet, it was brightly lit with the early fall sunlight pouring in.

It seemed smaller and more compact than the downstairs, but was somehow emptier. Like I said, there was trash in every doorway but the floors themselves seemed cleaner inside the rooms. Downstairs, some semblance of old chairs and tables remained, lying around in bits and pieces. But up here, there was no furniture, and no mysterious bookshelf with romantic antique books either.

Dad was brave enough to go peering into all the rooms while Mom and I decided to stick to exploring the one bedroom. There were plenty of spray-painted signatures, graffiti, pentagrams, and other lewd things drawn all over the walls.

However, I could not stop myself from thinking about what a nice bedroom this would have been back when the house was occupied by the living, when the people of the house looked out of the large windows and saw the rolling fields and forest in the distance, instead of a row of trees blocking off the road. I got a beautiful image in my mind of what it must have been like.

I also noticed that it was eerily quiet. Only our footsteps made a sound. Not even the house creaked in the slight breeze that drifted from room to room. Did I feel a cold spot? Mom was exploring the room and had drifted towards the corner. "Look, a door. Maybe this heads up to the attic," she said and disappeared around the corner, where there was a little inlet with a doorway. I followed quickly. She tried to turn the knob and pull it open. The door didn't budge. She dug her fingers into the frame and pulled on it. It didn't move a centimeter.

I decided to try my luck, pulling on the door with both hands until my knuckles were white. I heard whispering. I withdrew my hands right away.

It stopped. It was probably the sound of the door resisting pressure. But it was a creepy door anyway. There was something off about it. It was bright white, unlike anything else in the house, and the doorknob was perfectly black and intact. The whole thing felt cemented to the doorframe.

I heard more whispering—it was just the wind, I told myself. An image flashed through my mind of those phantom feet chasing us the other night. I imagined them belonging to old "Walter" himself and could just picture him standing there now, waiting on the other side of this door. The image somehow disturbed me and made me smile at the same time. I stepped away from the door quickly and decided to let it go for now.

"What a weird door," Mom said, cocking her head to one side.

"Yeah, it's freaky," I agreed, backing away from it some more. I put my hand on the wall as I turned the corner and felt something sharp puncture my skin.

"Ouch!" I cried out. My parents both jumped in surprise and then came to my rescue. I looked down at my hand and saw that a big piece of white wood was jutting out of my right index finger.

"Stand still, I got it," Mom said, taking my hand.

"Well, that's good," Dad said as Mom dug her nails into my finger, trying to pry the splinter out. "You're probably infected with asbestos now. Are you okay?"

"Ah, it's bleeding a little," Mom said as the splinter came free and a dot of blood formed on my finger. I reluctantly put the finger in my mouth and sucked off the blood, the aftertaste of old white paint sticking to my tongue.

"Just war wounds," I said casually, looking at the door.

"This place is really cool, though, you guys," Dad said, gazing around. "I can't believe we found it."

"I know," I agreed, sighing.

"You really like it here, Nor," Dad said. "I can tell. Splinters and all."

I smiled.

"Yep. Now let's go, I'm freaked out," Mom said decisively, pushing past us and leaving the room. We inched our way back down those awful stairs and out of the house.

As we left, I circled the house again, taking some more photos. I thought I would try clearing my mind and letting in any impressions. I didn't consider myself to be sensitive, but then again, when did I ever have the opportunity to find out? I tried soaking in any signs or messages from beyond. All I kept getting was that we should leave and go far away.

I sat alone in my bedroom. Now it was cemented in my mind that whatever was in the house didn't want us there. I added it all up in my head—the splinter, being chased away, that awful feeling of being unwanted. It could have all been a coincidence. After all, old abandoned properties aren't exactly the friendliest or most inviting of places.

But what I had sensed there had followed me home. It was there in the room with me, this palpable awareness of intrusion into someone's world. Either my world or their world, but regardless, it was there.

I didn't know how to feel about that, but I could understand why. Inside the house there was graffiti everywhere. The infamous books and bookshelves that had been there were all stolen. Who knows what else in the house had been torn apart and taken away? The floor was littered with old magazines and newspapers, pieces of records and glass bottles—things that used to belong to real, living people. And no one cared.

If I wanted to be a professional ghost hunter and a responsible historian, I had to take responsibility for places like this. Someone had to stand up for Walter's House. Deep down I felt like I was somehow meant to discover that house. I just didn't know why, or what to do about it.

A few days later Dad told me that he had spoken to some people at work, and they had tried to open the attic door once, too, but couldn't pry it open for anything. They also said they had heard a few more stories about people seeing the ghost of a man in one of the attic windows—from those attic eyes that had been staring down at me. This was priceless new information and my ghost hunting journal was quickly filling up. I was utterly fascinated by all of it.

In short time I also came to the conclusion that, since the presence in the house was a man, I would just call him Walter. The house was, after all, Walter's House, and I liked that name anyway. I had various ideas running through my mind of who Walter might have been. The manor was built in the eighteenth century, the ghost lady had been wearing a Victorian dress, and from the looks of the rubble in the house, the last inhabitants had left sometime in the 1950s.

So from which era was Walter? He could have been a farmhand in the stable, or a worker in the tavern later in the 1800s. He could have been a young Civil War soldier lost on the front lines, or a soldier from either of the World Wars, or even from the Revolutionary War. Maybe he was just a regular guy. My young mind decided that regardless of time, Walter must have met a tragic end in order to be such a dramatically unfriendly and unwelcoming spirit.

A great part of my growing fascination was also with the house alone. I could almost have believed that the house was an entity unto itself, with its own private identity and conscience. Walter was just the ghost roaming inside its walls—just he and the house for eternity. Maybe it was a little bit of both. All I knew was that I couldn't see Walter, but I could see the house in all its glory. It was the physical manifestation of him.

I had read a lot of books and watched all of the television programs I possibly could that dealt with the paranormal, but I had never experienced the supernatural for myself until now. I had never humanized it before, and had to ask myself not only *who* Walter was, but *what* Walter was.

There are parapsychologists, ghost hunters, and all manner of people with an opinion on the subject that believe a structure itself retains energies and memories, and therefore, when people see ghosts they are seeing images or shadows from another time, mechanically playing themselves out over and over.

Others believe that ghosts can also be individual or intelligent entities that are able to communicate with us and sometimes even attach themselves to people or objects.

I half romanticized and half dreaded the idea that Walter and his entourage might have followed me home. I couldn't shake the feeling, though, that someone was listening in on my thoughts. I was so pleased to have this new world to sink my imagination into, but it was as if, from somewhere deep inside the house or between dimensions, he knew it.

Still, I allowed myself to daydream—at home, in school, and everywhere I went—about the life and times of Walter and the seasons the house had weathered. I planned my next trip and waited eagerly for my photos from the last one to develop.

Three: Waiting

The weather was now cold, and green was giving way to bright colors and then bareness. I was looking forward to a perfect Halloween, the magic of the season highlighted by my real encounters with the ghosts and goblins of the world.

Every time we passed an old house or a partially torn down barn on the road, I was reminded of Walter's House, and I wondered if there were any lost spirits wandering there, too. Suddenly the world was a much more interesting place.

We didn't always have time to explore Walter's House when we drove by, but I always got to have a good long look at it out of the car window. The attic eyes would stare back and take me in as well.

As we drove back and forth past the old place, and saw it slowly blending in with the graying October skies behind it, I made sure to at least nod a little hello.

Just in case someone really was watching.

When I got back the photos, I barely made it out of the store and into the car again before I tore open the envelope and scoured the contents. I held my breath as I looked at each new photo, anticipating that at any second the image of a ghost might jump out at me. At first glance, however, the photos returned only nice daytime shots of an old abandoned house and its dark interior. But maybe I just hadn't looked closely enough. That evening, I sat under the light in the living room and looked at each photo carefully.

In the fifth photo, which I had taken of the staircase, part of the living room on the right hand side was visible. In the back, towards the kitchen, I could just make out what looked like a white, slightly translucent arm. It looked like the sleeve of the left arm of a man's shirt, bunched or coming to a tight close at the cuff. From the looks of it, the man would have been pretty tall, unless he was floating. I jotted all of this down in my log book. I ran my finger over the supposed apparition in my picture. It only looked kind of real, and I wasn't entirely convinced it wasn't just an old curtain.

The next photos were also rather uneventful. I had tried to take some pictures of the outside of the house from the other side, where the sun porch had been. They again returned nothing except for interesting architectural forms.

In one of the pictures at the back of the house, I had included Mom slightly in the foreground. This way if anything did show up, I could test the size of an average person in proportion to the house and also the distinctness of a living person versus a shadowy figure—or a mere illusion.

Then there was one of the last photos in the pile, which I had taken of the side of the house facing toward the restaurant, where the attic windows always peered down at me. In the photo, the side of the porch was also visible. I looked it over, holding it in my right hand. I was about to set it down and go to the next one when I took my thumb off the corner of the picture and gasped, dropping it.

My hand clenched shut and I instinctively rubbed my fingers together. I looked at the photo with wide eyes. Down in the right corner where my finger had been, there was the clear and unmistakable image of a man sitting in the grass, facing the camera and leaning against the porch.

From his size, he appeared to be a young man and he was holding what looked like a bucket or a pan over his head, as if he were posing for a joke. The image was fuzzy, almost as if he was in motion when the photo was taken. I couldn't see any details.

I picked up the photo and examined it closely. All I could make out was that he looked like he had dark hair and wore a white shirt, suspenders, and blue or brown pants. I wrote all of this down in a hurry, my heart beating fast. The pot or bucket he had over his head even gleamed in the sunlight, which was beaming down from above and would have illuminated the metal—had it actually been there.

I stood up and placed the photograph even closer to the light. He was still there. I blinked. He was still there. I compared the picture to that of Mom. Obviously it wasn't her or Dad—he was too short to be Dad, but looked a little taller than Mom, and they had both been wearing completely different colors. It was him, there he was. I had captured the ghost on film.

I held my breath. This was Walter.

But it didn't make any sense. This person was in a playful stance, relaxed. The vibes I had gotten from the house indicated a much older, more intense authority. I had been stifled by the sense that I was to leave and never come back. But this guy was wearing a freaking bucket on his head. Was he calling my bluff? Maybe my magical psychic abilities were dead wrong.

I supposed this could have been a different person, but I had the overwhelming sensation that this was exactly who I was looking for—this was *the* Walter, staring back at me. The dark and aggressive energy hanging in the house could have been caused by his restlessness, or his adolescence, or maybe I just wasn't meant to understand.

I looked back at the other photo of the "sleeve." It actually looked similar enough to the slightly blurred shirt that Walter was wearing in the other photo. Maybe it was a real capture, and these were the same person. I concluded in my journal that there was only one male ghost and this *was* him.

Ever preoccupied with the ideas of magic and mystery, I believed that no matter how alone I was or how tedious daily life in the suburbs could be for a young lady, there was always the possibility of something more right around the corner. Needless to say, I had something to prove right in my hand: I had the photo.

Now I was left to ponder whether this was some type of communication from the spirit, or if it was just a coincidence—just the shadow playing itself out. It was at least one more shred of evidence that there was meant to be some special connection between me and the house.

But then came the big letdown. I showed the picture to Mom and she said she could only sort of see what I was talking about. I told her it was obvious and that Walter was right there. She nodded and said there was definitely something there. I was confused, and slightly embarrassed that it wasn't as obvious to her as it was to me. I kept pointing to the figure, plain as day, and she would assure me that she saw something but couldn't guarantee it was a person.

"I'm old and have bad vision, though," she joked, trying to reassure me.

On an unseasonably cold night later that week, Mom fell asleep on the sofa while waiting for Dad to call for a ride home, and I sat in a chair reading. There was no television in our living room and I would describe the atmosphere as calm. I was thinking of Walter in the back of my mind.

I was a girl, and my mind inevitably drifted off to its little fantasy world, where I drew up scenarios of me and Walter—really good friends—back in the old days.

We were taking a walk in the fields behind the restaurant, where there were picturesque rolling hills and horses running in the background.

I went back in time and stood in the upstairs bedroom next to Walter, looking out of the window exactly as I had in real life, gazing upon all that was ours...

The house was all mine and only I had the privilege of understanding it and understanding the ghost, Walter. I was the only one who had taken the time to really think about it. I imagined my small, insignificant self being ushered into the house as it used to stand, by a taller, stronger young man who was thrilled for me to be there. I pictured myself in that quiet domestic farm-life setting. I would never have that opportunity today, not with the world as it was, or the way I was.

As abruptly as my fantasies began to unfold, they broke apart again. My mind interrupted with the question, "Well, how did he die?" He was after all, long gone. I closed my eyes and tried to meditate on the thought but not be sad about it, a familiar tinge of emptiness forming in my chest. As

I relaxed a little and hummed to myself, concentrating on him, I went into a kind of trance.

I started to notice that the random swirling of colorful blotches behind my eyes was taking on shapes. Human forms. I didn't try thinking them up deliberately, they just manifested themselves. I saw the abstract image of a large group of men who were wearing uniforms of some kind, gathered around another uniformed man on the ground. I felt my hands gripping the sides of the chair.

The image grew more vivid as the men took hold of the man lying down and began to carry him away. They hoisted him up under his arms, his legs limp and dragging on the ground like he was injured or unconscious. I opened my eyes. The image was still there, almost projected onto the wall in front of me. I blinked and it was still there, like a fuzzy movie that had leaked from my mind and was now precipitating onto the wall.

All of a sudden, I could hear it, too—the footfalls of people walking through the mud and the delirious moaning and protesting of the injured man. It was as if his feet were dragging across the very carpet in my living room. As I started to panic, the image faded and was completely gone.

Yet the sound of them reverberated in my ears. I felt my heart start to pound as the impact of it hit me. I jumped up onto my toes so that my whole body was in the chair, frozen, and glanced at

Mom out of the corner of my eye. She was still fast asleep. It was freezing in the room.

I stayed completely still, my eyes darting around wildly as if I didn't quite believe it was really over yet. I looked back at the wall and it was just a white wall again. "What was that, what was that?" I whispered to myself, my chest heaving. I waited a few moments and took a deep breath.

It must have happened though. The magnitude of his voice had shaken the plates that were hanging on the wall, and I could still hear them vibrating.

When we finally got to drive past the house that night, my stomach was in knots. I looked up at it hesitantly through the line of trees. It stood there black and menacing. A low voice in my head said, "You *know.*"

Four: Falling

So I began to rethink my psychic abilities again. It could follow me home, but what did it—or he—want? I needed, yet again, to find a way to sort out my thoughts. I had no clue about what to do with the information I had been given, and didn't understand why it had been given to me. Okay, I wanted to be a big ghost hunter, but I was also just a fifteen year old girl. And I certainly couldn't tell anyone about what had happened without sounding nuts.

That night really changed everything.

All was quiet for a little bit. I hit a busy patch at school and was engrossed in schoolwork for a while. The more distance I put between me and the incidences of late, the more I was confused about whether what was happening was real or very much my own mind being over stimulated. I had been bouncing back and forth between excitement and hesitation. It was good for me to take a break.

Then, one night when the house was all quiet, I fell into a warm, comfortable sleep. Unfortunately, a bizarre nightmare followed. I was in the dirt-covered basement of Walter's House. It was pitch-black and I was aware of standing in the middle of the room, facing the wall and feeling completely vulnerable and afraid to move an inch or make a sound. I don't know how I got there and I couldn't have seen if the stairs were there because it was so dark.

I felt a presence on my right side. I turned my head slightly, and met the gaze of a tall, gray horse, that seemed to glow in the dark. It wasn't an exaggerated glowing, it just happened to be perfectly visible among all the blackness. It came to stand beside me, and I immediately noticed that its big left eye was a human eye. It was studying me with this big, blue eye and I held my breath in terror, yet felt compelled to lift my hand up and touch it.

I couldn't even see my hand in the dark and as I brought it up slowly to touch the horse's face, it caught my hand in its dry white teeth and bit down as hard as it could. Its gaze remained calm all the while, but I could feel the pressure as it clamped down, its hot, shallow breath blowing onto my forearm. It felt so real, time seemed to melt away as I tried to scream and pull away.

I woke up feeling tingly all over and unable to move. I was disoriented and frightened for a couple of minutes until the feeling came back to my arms and legs. I sat up, looking around the room for any intruders, but I was alone. I held up my right hand and looked at it. In the faint glow of my night light, it looked like there were teeth marks slowly fading from the palm and back of my hand. I still couldn't feel my hand even though the feeling had been restored everywhere else.

I smelled my hand. It smelled musty, like a basement. Tears formed in my eyes as a chill ran down my back and I swallowed the urge to panic.

Maybe it was his way of reminding me that he was still there. "What do you want from me?" I whispered, exhausted at trying to analyze his strange sense of humor.

There was certainly some discrepancy between the happy ghost picture and the experiences I was having. I was convinced I was dealing with a single entity, Walter. But this way of communicating wasn't working. I had no idea what it meant. When I thought of Walter, I felt— well—love, in my own strange way. I felt a sense of responsibility and obligation, and there was, for sure, something going on between me and the house. But I wasn't about to let it take me for a ride.

On a quiet November afternoon, Mom allowed me to approach the house and go inside alone. She figured I had been in there enough times to be able to take care of myself. She decided to read in the car while I did some exploring on my own.

I walked up to the house. I approached it with new poise. I had nothing to lose and shoved all the doubts to the back of my mind when I saw the spot where Walter had appeared in the photo. I told myself I should just keep picturing that goofy guy with the pot on his head if I got too scared.

I walked around to the porch and could no longer see my mother's car. That was just a little daunting. But finally, after so many weeks, I felt like I belonged there. There was, in fact, a mutual recognition. Like a shy dog, the house had finally accepted me. I had earned its trust.

I looked through the doorway and a chill went through me. In a fleeting thought, I wished desperately that I had lived in that house once when everyone inside was still alive, and I felt like Walter or the house or whoever was there felt the same way, too.

Tape recorder in hand, it was time to go in and make some real, personal contact. I climbed onto the porch and approached the door. For some reason I hesitated, not sure if I really wanted to know after all. If I got no voices or answers, I would be disappointed. There had been too many real boys that had never returned my calls or picked up the phone. I don't know if I could handle an all-pervading, time traveling spirit not answering me either.

The only time I had ever touched anything in the house was when I put my hand on the doorframe to the attic. I had never picked up anything or even kicked something aside with my foot. This time, however, I tenderly reached out with a flat, open hand and placed it against the front doorframe, feeling the splintered wood and a cold rusty nail resting underneath my palm. I let my hand take in every sensation.

Without my parents around, I figured I could try to speak to him out loud and not be embarrassed. "Hello, Walter's House."

Well, this was already embarrassing. "I mean you no harm and just want to come inside for a minute. I appreciate you letting me visit you so many times."

That really must have sounded ridiculous. But immediately, I felt my chest growing as my lungs filled up with fresh air. A chilly breeze blew from behind me and pushed me gently into the house. I held out the tape recorder and turned it on. I wasn't scared at all. "I just want to ask you a few questions. Walter, are you here? Are you the ghost who haunts this house?"

I waited and heard nothing, as expected. I walked into the living room, looking around, and took a peek at the old magazines on the floor. There were tattered brown home improvement magazines, old Reader's Digests, and some wall calendars with cheesy painted nature scenes on them—very domestic. All of them came from the 1940s or 50s, around the time when the house must have been abandoned. I wondered if the house or if Walter ever missed people being around. Maybe the bitterness and anger stemmed from loneliness. Could a haunted house actually be bitter?

It was noticeably colder the further I stepped inside, but the air was fresh, not as musty as it had been in the warmer weather. "Why was this house abandoned?" I asked slowly, allowing time for anyone to answer. "Who are you, Walter? When did you live? How did you die?" I spaced each question out carefully. I felt suddenly uncomfortable standing alone in the middle of the room like that, especially if I looked over to the doorway to the basement.

But it was temporary. It's just Walter here, I thought. "Walter, I just want to help you." I felt really stupid talking out loud like this, but I could see the image of him being dragged across my living room floor. That was intimate. But why?

"Walter, if you're there, will you please show me a sign?"

I stood still, just breathing in and out for a few moments. Then I saw something from the corner of my eye. I looked quickly, adrenaline kicking in.

It was my breath. I breathed out again, and noticed that I could now see my breath.

Then, a door or shutter unexpectedly slammed from somewhere upstairs. I couldn't remember if there had been a gust of wind or not. It wasn't out of the question. My hands were shaking a little but I remained where I was. "Walter?" I asked timidly, my voice cracking. It was getting colder. There were no other noises for a few seconds. It dawned on me that regardless of ghosts, there could always be living people lurking somewhere on the property.

Then I heard a long, slow creak across the floor directly above me. "Oh god," I barely whispered. I was afraid and insanely hopeful at the same time. I braced myself, ready to dash out the door if I needed to. It was only a few feet away, but the staircase was also there. I would have to run past it to escape.

I prayed this was all on the tape recorder. Otherwise no one would ever believe me.

After a few throbbing heartbeats, I inched my way over to the door and backed out onto the porch, ready to jump off and run. I looked up the stairs, wondering if he might appear at any moment, expecting to see a leg step into my line of vision, bringing my ghost with it. My whole body was shaking.

But no one came. He was definitely there, though, just a few steps away and I could feel him all over me. He wanted me to know he was there. That was enough for now. I turned off the tape recorder and got the hell out of there.

"Any luck?" Mom asked me from the safety of the car.

"I heard something slam upstairs," I gushed breathlessly, "right when I asked for the ghost to show me a sign. And then I heard creaking like someone walking across the floor! Did you hear anything out here?"

"No, nothing. I didn't hear anything out here, I swear. Did you get it all on tape?"

"I frickin' hope so," I answered. As we pulled away, I rewound the tape and then eagerly pressed the play button, my hands still trembling.

"Okay, listen," I said.

We both listened. The tape recorder was pretty cheap and mostly picked up only the air whirring loudly through the microphone. However, my steps on the hard wood floor could be heard over the constant "whoosh" in the background. I listened carefully, turning the volume all the way up.

I could hear myself breathing on the recorder and then asking questions. It occurred to me that Mom was being let in on what was, to me, a pretty personal conversation. I guess I didn't really care, though. I was too ready to find out if there was anything on the tape.

So far there were no answers to any of my questions. No ghostly dissertations here. Maybe I hadn't waited long enough for him to conjure up the energy to speak, or maybe I was talking over him—assuming he was talking at all. The whooshing sound changed a few times, getting higher or lower in pitch as I moved around and changed directions.

When it got to the part where something slammed shut upstairs, I got really excited because it *did* register on the recording.

Then I heard myself say, "Walter?" I gulped and listened further. Mom put her head closer to the recorder while still watching the road. The floor creaked again and then I thought I heard a different noise, something low and faint in the background. I stopped the tape.

"Did you hear that?" I asked her. I could feel my pupils dilating and the hairs rising on the back of my neck.

"No, I didn't," she admitted. "Play it again, I missed it. All I heard was the wind."

I rewound it a little too far and played it back, waiting for it to get to that part again.

"Walter?" my voice on the recording said.

Then I heard a very faint voice.

"I heard that!" Mom exclaimed, slowing down the car suddenly.

"Shhh," I cautioned.

The creak came. "Oh god," I whispered on the tape. Then came the voice again. It sounded like the same thing it had said before but I couldn't tell for sure.

I rewound it again.

"Put it on the half speed thing," Mom suggested. I placed the speed counter at half speed.

We waited again, listening to the distorted sound of the air going through the recorder.

"Walter?" my deep, distorted voice asked.

Then the barely audible voice responded, "Hello?"

"What?" I shouted at the tape recorder. Mom pulled over suddenly near a fenced in field where horses were munching on some grass near the road. They watched our car lazily as we sat there in complete shock. I stopped the tape, placed it back at regular speed, and played it again.

"Walter?"

Now I could hear a male voice answering normally, "Hello?"

I listened to the creak, heard myself respond. Then I heard the second word, very soft. "Nora?"

"Oh my Jesus Christ," Mom uttered, shrinking away from the tape recorder. "I don't believe that at all. I don't believe it."

I stopped the tape and just stared at her blankly. "You heard that?"

"Uh, yeah!" she said, putting the car in gear again and speeding off down the road. I rewound it again and heard the same thing, this time coming through clearly.

"Someone was saying 'hello,' and then they said your name. I heard it plain as day," Mom confirmed.

He said my name, I thought. I played it one more time.

"Walter?"

"Hello?"

"Oh god..."

"Nora?"

This time, my Mom did not brush it off. She was worried, and she let me know it. "This is all pretty cool, but it freaks me out. I mean, this might not be a good thing, if the ghost knows your name."

"Yes, yes, I agree," I told her as we sat at the table, eating dinner while Dad was at work. For the record, he thought we were both crazy when we told him about the voice, and claimed he heard nothing when we played the tape for him. "But I'm also excited. I mean, *I* went to the ghost, I instigated something."

I was floating on a cloud. This was easily the coolest thing that had ever happened to me.

"Maybe I've watched too many horror movies in my life time, but Nora, I have never heard of a ghost actually making personal contact unless something bad was about to happen."

Something about that statement made me feel uncomfortable in my seat. Not just that this conversation was completely strange, but also, she had a good point. She didn't even know I was investing so much emotion into this, and it's true that I wasn't being cautious.

It occurred to me that even though there could very well be a friendly ghost named Walter somewhere on the property, I—as a vulnerable teenage girl—could have been contacting *anything* that was able to force its way into my conscience and pretend to be nice. Anyone could be channeling me through my desire to contact

Walter so badly. This could be much more serious than I thought.

Still, I replied, "But I believe the spirit is good."

And I did, but I was more confused than ever—the vision, the dream, all of it. What did it all mean? There was still so much to sort out, for the sake of my safety and my sanity.

Looking at the situation as a whole—going over all of the notes in my logbook and examining all of the evidence—I decided there were two possibilities. There was, I believed, one ghost I was making contact with on a consistent basis that was allowing me into his world after some reluctance. This was my first choice—Walter as I imagined him, a lonely spirit able to contact me because I was encouraging him to.

Or there was the second option—that whatever I had contacted was a negative and manipulative force that was playing a game with me and invading my space at home.

Everyone who ever worked at the restaurant came in random contact with spirits, but it seems I was having a "relationship" with one, whatever that was supposed to mean. The thought of what a living adult male having any kind of relationship with a fifteen-year-old girl would imply in modern society also made me feel a little strange.

But I was too intrigued, too enchanted with what was happening, to stop.

My only wish was that he wasn't much older than me and if it turned out he was, that his intentions were benign. That way, maybe what was going on in my mind and what he wanted from me was the same thing.

Mom calmed down about it after a few days and let it go. I hadn't sat up in bed yet with my head spinning around, so she must have figured everything was going to be alright. In fact, my dreams had been very pleasant and I had slept well, which was rare back then.

Then something very interesting happened. Apparently, Walter wanted to be a gentleman about things after all and saw fit to introduce himself to Dad.

One afternoon, Dad had to go down into the wine cellar at work to get a few bottles for some customers. This was everyone's least favorite task, as the basement seemed to have been the only place in the restaurant not renovated in the last several hundred years. It also seemed to be the place where the most ghostly activity happened during business hours.

He was apparently selecting wines when he felt like someone was standing behind him, a man to be specific. He wasn't sure how he knew it was a man, just that it was that kind of a presence.

I knew the feeling.

He waited for the guy standing there to say something or move, thinking it was a colleague of his, but instead he said he waited a second and felt like something was not right. Then he felt a heavy, cold hand come to rest on his shoulder. He whirled around to see who it was, but of course there was no one there.

Dad said that in all the time he had worked there, and for all the scary stories he had ever heard, nothing could have prepared him for the icy chill that ran through him at that moment. He leapt up the stairs, almost dropping the bottles, and vowed never to go in the basement alone again.

When he came home and told us that story, I had to smile on the inside. The hand on the shoulder trick—a classic. I knew it had to be my Walter.

Five: The Door Opens

It was now well into winter and the ground was gleaming bright white with so many snowfalls. It was unusual for it to snow so much in Maryland in a given year. I stood on the porch of Walter's House, rocking back and forth on my heels, with such a feeling of romance in my heart that I thought my chest would burst.

For the first time, I could see that I was not the only one captivated by Walter and his house. There were several sets of old and fresh footprints leading in and out of the doorway. For some reason, a wave of jealousy crept up my throat and I felt it tighten, as if I had caught them in the act. It made me wonder if I was not the only close friend of Walter, but only for a second before I came to my senses and got back to reality.

The house had taken on a new, magical quality. It was as quiet as ever there and everything was still, hushed under the weight of layers of snow. The snow was nearly as deep inside the house as it was outside, and a fresh, freezing wind whipped through the rooms from window to window.

Upstairs, the bare branches of trees—icicles forming on the ends like droplets on a runny nose—intruded into the rooms. As I went inside and looked around, I felt, as usual, like I was being watched, but this time by someone who was very happy to see me.

It was under these cold and frozen circumstances that I was finally able to pry open the attic door.

Actually, when I walked into the room where the attic door was located, there were already sets of footprints following my exact path. Some other adventurers—and judging from the size of the prints, some big, strong, male adventurers—had also found the attic door and tried to open it. But without success. There was no sign of snow being moved away from the door as it opened and it looked like it hadn't budged at all. The footsteps stopped in front of the door and then came back.

I took hold of the door handle. There is a theory that a spirit dwells in one specific part of a house, like as its home base, even if it can move around to different places. Why did I have the sneaking suspicion that this was his private hideout where he watched the world?

"Walter, can I come in?" I whispered. Mom was downstairs with Dad, having a look around and chatting as usual. I was alone and not scared at all.

The door didn't move. I did have gloves on, so my grip was pretty shoddy. I took off my glove and wrapped my bare hand around the icy latch. It was a shock of cold. "Please?" I asked. "Come on, let me in." I thought real hard about wanting the door to open, seeing again the form of Walter in my mind, hovering on the other side with one hand on the knob and one hand on the frame— ready to open the door. "Please," I said with my eyes closed.

I waited several seconds, pulling on the knob slightly until, with a small crack, the latch lifted up and the door swung easily towards me.

It was just that simple. It kind of fell open, light as a feather. My jaw dropped.

I looked up into the darkness of the attic, little cracks of light peaking through the shingles on the roof, and felt like I was being given entry into the beating heart of the house. My worries about the nature of Walter left me. I had earned the right to be a part of what was happening here, and for no other reason than being a patient, understanding person. I had reached out to the house in a way no one else had ever dared.

With this in mind, I easily climbed the stairs of what would normally be a mind-bendingly terrifying, dark and haunted attic. There were only about five or six steps to go. I went up about three until I was eyelevel with the floor. This floor was not the original one. Holes and patches in the wood revealed another floor several feet below, almost level with the bedroom. This was puzzling.

I turned to my left to look through the famous watching windows. The newer floor was actually level with the bottom ledge of those windows. How odd, I thought. But this still left plenty of space in the attic for trash and debris to pile up.

The biggest regret I had about going into the attic was that I found a number of old-fashioned, dusty scrolls of paper wound on wooden reams lying around, and I *didn't* look at them. I think I was so afraid to touch them—in case they would break or I would get dirt all over myself—that I may have missed the opportunity to discover a wealth of information about the house and its former inhabitants. They were huge and looked so heavy, and I somehow had this inclination that I was not supposed to touch them. So I just left them alone.

Instead, I looked around, not going up any further, but pivoting in my spot on the third step, just in case I did have to run from bats or something. I took some photos, and stood there in a trance-like state for several minutes. I started to feel extra cold, as if all the heat were draining away from my body. I no longer heard my parents downstairs. It was like everything stopped all of a sudden and every particle, illuminated by the bleak light coming in through the eye windows, seemed to suspend in mid-air. I could see it all, and it was like the whole room was wrapping itself around me. I took in every inch of it, knowing he was there somewhere.

"Where are you?" I asked softly, coming out of my daze. "I want to see you." I stood there for another few minutes and then shook my head clear of the dizziness, turned, closed the door gently behind me, and went back downstairs.

I couldn't wait to tell my parents that I was able to open the attic door.

"No way, Nora!" Dad said, very excited. "What did you find in there?"

"Cool old scrolls, lots of trash. It's dark up there. Your basic attic pretty much," I explained.

"Hey, let's go up real quick," he said to Mom.

"Sure, let's go see. Honey, will you be okay to wait a minute down here by yourself?" she asked me.

"Absolutely, take your time," I said, watching them head up.

I listened to their footsteps above me and then stepped outside onto the porch. I looked at the old banisters, barely able to hold up the slowly collapsing roof. Regardless of anything going on with ghosts, it occurred to me how lucky I was to have such an opportunity as this. My life was nothing so far if not unique.

They came back down after a while and said they had managed to open the door but were too scared to go in. As we were walking away from the house, my footsteps crunching in the snow, I looked back up to the attic windows. There had been so many times already when I had just expected to see someone there. The feeling was so strong, but of course, I didn't see anyone and told myself not to be disappointed. If Walter wanted me to see him, he would show himself.

I wanted to see a ghost so badly, I could just taste it on the tip of my tongue. He was right there. Come on, Walter. Where are you?

I stopped and said to Mom, loud enough for the house to be within listening distance, "I just wish I could see the ghost. I just wish he would appear *one* time. Not jump out of a closet and scare the crap out of me, but just be there."

"I know you do, Nora," Mom said, kind of seriously. "I just don't think the ghost wants to scare you. Maybe he can sense that though, and I'm sure one day you'll see him. He knows your name."

"Seeing a ghost would be too cool," Dad added. "And he didn't say anything. You guys made all that up in your heads." He smiled.

"You deserve to see Walter," Mom said, ignoring him and surprising me. "With all the time you've spent at this place, you could write a book about it." She turned and I could hear her feet crunching away. I didn't take my eyes off of those windows.

I looked, finally, over to the porch where he had shown up in my photo. That spot was all covered in snow and footprints. Biting my lip, I sighed, rolled my eyes at myself, and followed them back to the car.

We started to drive away. We pulled out of the parking lot, taking our usual left, and were about to pass the house one more time. It should be stated again that it was a gray day—not too sunny and not too cloudy. There was no glare from the sun and the sky was clear. The trees were bare so that we, and all who passed it, had a clear view of the house (aside from the pines). Mom was in the driver's seat and I was in the back on her side.

I remember a feeling which at the time I could only describe as a swirling feeling start to erupt in my stomach. I put one hand on the back of the headrest in front of me and looked up at the house.

"STOP," I said deliberately. Mom, without hesitation, slowed the car down until we were almost standing still, and we both looked up. She leaned over the steering wheel, letting out a short gasp.

"Look," she said. Dad was trying to lean over from the passenger side and look up at the same spot we were concentrating on.

We were all staring up at the attic windows, about ten yards away from us at this point. There are no words to adequately describe what I saw and how it made me feel at that moment and for years to come. Without any doubt, there was Walter looking down at us.

I saw a man leaning, with both of his hands on the windowsill, out of the attic window on the right side, his left. He was looking directly at us.

The dizzy swirling feeling shot outward through my whole body as our eyes met, like an adrenaline rush multiplied by one hundred. I held my breath, simply feeling my heart jolt into a burst of palpitations, blood rushing to my ears.

I looked down at his hands, holding onto the windowsill. He was not transparent at all, but completely solid like a living person, only he was almost a uniform white color. He was bent over a little in order to fit his upper body out the window, and I could tell he had a smaller stature, like the young man in the picture I took.

I calculated that if he was standing on the original floor, about three feet from the windows, he must have been only a little bit taller than me.

He was wearing a white shirt that gathered at the cuffs. I could just see the top of his pants and what looked like suspenders. His clothes looked worn even though they were as white as he was, but there was a slight beige hue tinting the folds. I could not, though, see any of the details of his face because it was so pale white.

I saw his face, with short curly hair and wisps of bangs sticking out in front, but I could never describe it. I just understood that he was looking down at me.

Knowing that he had heard my request and then honored it was like nothing less than Christmas morning. His stance was almost one of surprise, like he was shocked that we could see him, too, but also hopeful—like he was trying to make himself as visible as possible.

I asked very quickly, "Mom, what is it that you see?"

"A man at the window," she answered flatly.

"Leaning out and looking at us?" I asked breathlessly.

"Correct," she answered in the same flat tone.

"I don't see him," Dad said, barely above a whisper. "Which window?"

"Look at the attic window on the right," my Mom said cautiously, without turning her head, as if we were looking at a deer that we didn't want to scare away.

"I don't see him," Dad insisted, but we were already passing the house. Walter's head turned slowly to follow us until we were completely out of sight.

"Should I back up?" she asked me, still too dazed to react.

"No," I said. I didn't want to ruin the moment if he was gone.

We drove in silence for a few seconds. We turned left again to go down a new road, and passed the other side of the house in the distance. I took a last look at it until it was gone behind the trees.

"Nora," Mom asked evenly, "was that a ghost or a real person?"

My eyes and throat started to itch a little, like I was going to cry. "Well," I answered, breathing heavily, "I was just in the attic. I was gonna' tell you, the floor in the attic goes all the way up to the window. There is no way that anyone could lean out the window unless they were lying on their stomach and pushing themselves outward. But that's not the original floor."

She nodded, understanding what I meant.

"It looked like a ghost, too, didn't it?" she asked in disbelief, her voice coming back to life.

"What did it look like?" Dad asked, excited, shifting in his seat. "I looked but I didn't see anything! You guys must be more sensitive or something, I swear I didn't see anyone!"

She described to him with fervor exactly what I had seen. "And he was looking right at us, like a completely normal person. If he hadn't been so white he would have looked just like a real person standing there."

"Yeah, but what did he look like? I mean, what was his expression?" Dad asked eagerly.

She thought for a second. "He looked, like, startled, like he was surprised to see us. I guess he also looked curious, like he was interested in us."

Every word made my chest tighten a little more.

"How old did he look?" I asked, my voice quivering.

"I don't know. I couldn't really...tell." She paused. "I don't think I can drive anymore."

They got out and switched. She couldn't stop talking about how incredible the experience had been. And after a minute or two of trying desperately to swallow the lump in my throat, my chest lightened up and I found myself laughing with joy. This happened in movies and books, not in real life, not to me.

It *was* freaking Christmas morning—*I saw the ghost.* I saw Walter.

After an hour of painstakingly writing out my observations and how it all happened, my hand had cramped badly and yet I still had more to write. I tried to convey the caliber of the experience—the fact that Mom and I had corroborated seeing the same exact thing without telling each other too much information.

Dad was disappointed but he was happy for us. He talked about how cool it was over and over, but he wasn't nearly as touched because he hadn't seen Walter, he hadn't interacted with the ghost.

Plus, nobody knew I loved Walter. That would have been an interesting one to explain.

There was no way I could get to sleep in the state I was in. I lay awake, fantasizing about what my life would be like in Monkton, Maryland, had I lived over a hundred years ago.

I heard my parents talking as if we had just seen a celebrity. "We should go up there at night again sometime. We should take some flashlights and check it out in the dark. Wouldn't that be fun? We saw a real ghost. That's incredible. I can't wait to go back."

"Sounds good to me. I can't believe you saw one either. I just can't get my head around all this. We're having the Hendricks over next week. I bet they're up for it. Why don't we see if they want to have a little adventure that night?"

"Hell, yeah. I know they're up for that kind of thing. Let's do it. I'll bet Nora will get a kick out of it, too. She really loves that house."

"She certainly is having a good time. I think it's pretty harmless after all. I'll call them tomorrow and ask them."

It was like all doubts about the nature of the ghost had been wiped away. Everyone was a fan, but I was still the biggest fan.

Six: Walter

In one week, I was back there in the dark—around nine at night this time—in the snow, with a new flashlight, my parents and their two friends. This was just a little awkward. I admit that I was probably raised around an unusual bunch.

This time we had parked across the street, away from the restaurant, and walked towards the house from the front. The ice covering the ground and the house glistened in the moonlight, and it was more attractive and inviting than I had ever seen it.

"Nora's a real expert on the house," Mom explained to the Hendricks. I had told all of my stories on the way there and didn't want to be bothered with it anymore. I wanted to go off by myself and leave them to chatter loudly and joke around without me. I wanted to go find Walter.

I had a feeling like an electric current buzzing through and around me. It was coming from the house, as if he had been waiting for me. I tried to make some distance between us and get into the house ahead of them, but they followed right behind me.

The Hendricks looked around, marveling at the structure and all of its piles of stuff on the floor. Most of it had been snowed upon and was invisible but some old records and magazines still stuck out. "Jon, we should take something with us," Holly suggested. He agreed. I hadn't thought of that before. I was always too afraid to take anything away from there. It just seemed disrespectful.

But after she suggested it, it dawned on me that it might be a great idea for me to take something. The current, or whatever it was, droned away inside of me, alerting me and urging me as if to say, "Have your pick of whatever you want." Now that I knew what Walter looked like, I could picture him standing there, hands in his pockets, rocking back and forth while waiting for me to take something—anything, it was all mine.

Stepping past the door leading to the Stairway to Hell, an unseen force seemed to turn me and I shone my flashlight through that dreaded doorway to the basement. The Mason jars glistened on the shelf. There were a bunch of them, intact, unbroken—dusty but otherwise fine. I walked over and examined them. Up close they were stained brown and smelled ancient. I looked over them and spotted a small jar that looked appealing. I picked that one up and placed it gently into my coat pocket. A piece of Walter to take home with me.

"Thank you," I said out loud, feeling the jar weighing down my pocket. It reminded me again of long ago domestic settings that were now just a distant and remote part of the house's memory.

Then I turned around again to see my parents and the Hendricks leaned over the snowy piles of rubble, sorting through old papers and other junk.

I walked towards the kitchen where there was a small patch of floor that hadn't been touched by the snow. A folded up yellowed newspaper was poking out from beneath some unidentifiable trash. I bent down and picked it up.

Oh wow, I thought as I looked at the top of the page. This paper was dated Friday, November 13, 1944. What an incredible coincidence, I said to myself.

My assumption was that Walter had lived many generations before 1944, and the time of these papers and Mason jars, but he had still haunted them. The discovery of the newspaper was pretty wild, for any haunted house. Once again, I knew with absolute resolution that it was meant for me.

I glanced over the stories on the page, in case any might be significant to my quest. Nothing special. I folded it up and tucked it very gently underneath my arm.

"I'm going upstairs," I told them.

They stopped and looked at me like, "In the dark—are you crazy?"

"Okay, be careful Nor," Dad warned.

"Can she go up there by herself?" Jon asked him.

"Oh, she's been up there a hundred times. She knows the place in and out." He turned to me. "We'll be right up, I'm sure," he assured me.

"Okay." Yeah great, I thought. I hurried up as carefully as I could. I just had an overpowering feeling someone special was waiting there for me.

I walked, without minding my steps or being cautious at all, into the bedroom. It was very quiet and peaceful. The moonlight came shining in on the one side closest to the attic door, leaving only the far corners in darkness. As I made my way toward the windows to have a look out, I jumped as I saw out of the corner of my eye that the attic door was standing wide open.

He was there somewhere, the spirit unleashed upon the house. My adrenaline shot up and then came down again quickly, as I knew with relief that it was only Walter.

I stood facing the attic door when I had the sensation from behind me that someone was in the room. All of the talking and laughing from downstairs faded away, and in the dropping temperature my breath escaped my mouth in great billowing clouds. I could feel someone there behind me the way you know when there's someone in the next room, or someone looking over your shoulder. You don't have to see them— your most primordial human instincts tell you someone's there. I had an instant rush of fear and elation. After a few seconds I calmed down and relaxed.

That's not to say I wanted to turn around, but who else could it have been? In the moment, of all things I could have wondered—such as, was there a scary homicidal drifter hiding in the room with me—I suddenly asked myself if I looked okay.

I turned slowly, expecting that someone was standing literally right behind me. Instead, there was no one there, at least not in the line of sight of my flashlight. So in one of my bravest moves ever, I clicked off the flashlight. Everything went dark for a few seconds and I stood frozen still, letting my eyes look around without moving my head.

As my eyes adjusted to night vision, I could see something directly ahead of me in the far corner. It looked like the black silhouette of a man leaning against the wall, blacker than the darkness around him.

I thought, no way. Opening and closing my eyes again, he was still there. His shoulders were sort of shrugged up and his arms were folded over, like he was nervous or shrinking away from me.

Startled, I gasped and put my hand over my mouth. The figure straightened up so abruptly that I took a step back. He looked like he was either going to rush forward or run away. I held my breath and felt all the heat leaving the core of my body.

Then he took a step forward and Walter seemed to materialize in front of me—from a black form to a nearly solid person standing there, with two wide, filmy eyes staring back at me. He looked exactly as he had the day I had seen him from the car.

I could still never completely describe his face and could never say for sure how old he really was. I could see his brown eyes and vaguely recall the rest of him. He was like the young man in the picture after all. Those pale eyes were so piercing and strange, though, that I lost the rest of him in concentrating on them.

It seemed he was only a little taller than me, as I had thought, and his curly hair was muted white against his white skin. He was less than five feet away from me.

He didn't dart away after all, but relaxed his shoulders and put his arms down at his sides. He moved very slowly, first lowering his giant eyes to his hands and then reaching a hand out, palm facing outward, more like he was showing me his hand than wanting me to take it.

What would his hand feel like? I took off my glove and took one step forward, reached out, hovered there for a moment, and then placed my small hand flat on his, fingertips first. It was like laying my hand on a block of ice. But I could still feel softness underneath and recognized the touch of human skin. I gasped and withdrew my hand quickly.

"Sorry," I whispered. He closed his hand and took it back, like he was holding something. I looked up into his face again. He was still peering directly into my eyes. My heart pulled in my chest, the electric current whirring through me.

Sadly, I could see in those eyes that he was not living but very dead. Though this was so obvious, the surge of disenchantment rolled over me like a dull, heavy weight. There was something separate and glassy about them. They were yellowed at the corners and there were traces of warmth and life in them that must have existed once upon a time, but were just memories now.

Still, I smiled. The corners of his pale mouth turned up. I don't know how long we stood there, staring at each other. Neither of us said anything, even though I had so many questions and my head was reeling with things I wanted to say. I had a feeling like this was it, I probably wouldn't see him again, and he knew it, too. I focused on taking in the moment.

After a few seconds of silence, I could hear everyone making their way up the stairs. Walter broke his gaze once, looked toward the doorway, and then looked back at me, his head moving mechanically like a doll's.

We could hear them talking loudly. They were upstairs already and looking around near the other room. I glanced around quickly to see if any one of them was looking in at us, and when I looked back, he was fading away. "Walter," I said. He faded until there was just a static appearance to the air he had been occupying, like the little particles you see inside your eyelids when you close your eyes.

In another second, he was completely gone from sight, but still there.

Jon came down the hall just then and shined his flashlight into the room. "Jesus!" he shouted when he saw me, cutting into the silence and nearly falling backwards onto the floor. "Oh my...you scared the you-know-what outta' me," he said, catching himself and stepping into the room. I felt a cold block of air move through me toward the attic door. My parents and Holly were suddenly in the doorway.

"See anything, Nor?" Mom asked.

"Nope," I answered. I was annoyed and still spellbound at the same time. I put my glove back on and thrust my hand into my pocket, feeling the coldness of the Mason jar. A sense of urgency jolted through me and I understood how important it was for me to take that jar.

Outside, I stood alone in the dark and looked up at the house, trying to squint and see into the attic windows. He was there somewhere, looking down at me. What did he want from me? I was filled with a strange mixture of joy and sadness.

I saw no more shapes or figures that night, but waved up to the windows anyway. In my head, I kept asking him what it was he wanted and what I could possibly do for him. The image of him lingered in my mind. I didn't know it, but that was the last time I would ever see him or the house again.

Seven: The Accident

We bought a new car for me. It was time to start learning to drive. Dad drove himself to work. Winter was over and I had a thousand projects to finish for school. Before I knew it, the snow had melted and it was jacket weather again. Flowers were growing and leaves were slowly sprouting on the trees, turning the world green again.

Walter was always on my mind. I felt like he was with me all the time, but in an abstract way, not so aggressively as before.

The Mason jar and the newspaper were tucked away safely in a special bag so they wouldn't get damaged further. I hid them in my closet. My two little pieces of the house were with me whenever I needed to go there in my mind.

I really have no explanation, though, as to why I didn't physically make it back there for so many months.

One day there was a horrific drunk driving accident on the property of the restaurant. Dad had rushed home from work that day to tell us about how Walter's House had been involved.

A lady was driving drunk early in the morning while it was still dark outside. She was driving on the road that passed the restaurant when she blacked out at the wheel. Just as she was coming around the turn in front of the house, she hit the guardrail—which then sailed through the air and landed *on* the porch of Walter's House— and plowed through the trees. From the angle she was coming, she should have rammed straight into the house.

But instead, Dad explained, at the last second, the car turned left at a sharp angle, then turned right again and came to a stop in the parking lot near the back of the house. If we didn't believe him, he told us, we could go see the tire marks in the grass for ourselves. The police were baffled. It was as if a phantom pair of hands had taken the wheel at the last second and saved the house and the driver's life. The lady was injured but alive.

Old, shy Walter was still at work protecting his property. Dad said it was easily one of the most amazing things he had ever seen.

After hearing this story I went to my room, knelt at the bed, and looked at the jar and the newspaper. Walter had let me take them, and he would do anything to keep that house intact. I rolled the dusty jar around in my hands. Even my Mom remarked later how incredible it was that I got away with some of his things. It was mine to keep, a piece of the house that I was allowed to have, when no one else could break that barrier.

Some people had taken things of course, but I had been given something priceless.

Unfortunately, the accident attracted a lot of local attention to both the restaurant and the house. Walter's House had stood there next to the road for decades—for all who passed by to see—and had successfully evaded everyone's attention for so long. Now it had been found out. The house was deemed unsafe and unnecessary, and it was scheduled to be torn down.

Mom and I desperately wanted to get out there one more time before they demolished it, but Dad, also busy at work with springtime in full swing, did not know when they were planning on tearing it down. We scheduled a time and drove out there, but when we got there, the house was already gone.

It was bizarre. It had seemed like an instant between the time we heard the news and the time that I was standing there in front of a grassy lawn.

There was not a single solitary trace of the house, and the hole where the basement had been was filled in and was already grown over with grass. It looked like nothing had ever been built there. The most significant course of events in my young life had taken place there, in what was now just air.

My only consolation prize was the unnaturally green grass. The ground there was fertile and I believed that was no coincidence.

I stood there remembering how I had promised myself that I would help Walter in any way I could. There were many unanswered questions, but I tried to reason with myself. The house was gone, and maybe he was gone with it, too—finally resting, which is what would be best for him. He also must have known something was coming, and had intended for me to take those objects away so that he could have something to remain with in this world.

Of course, he could still just be quite busy haunting the restaurant and the rest of the property. Maybe he wasn't gone at all, just relocated. But I would always treasure that house.

I had a moment of silence for Walter and his house, and turned around toward the restaurant. If he was still in there somewhere, I could go see him whenever I wanted. The thought made me laugh a little, like he was a pet I couldn't keep and had to give back to the pet store.

That comforted me as I looked back and forth from the restaurant to where Walter's house used to be. All of my loneliness and naïve longing could be summed up in this one gaping, flagrantly empty space. This beautiful house—my special place—was gone.

The End of Something

It is not there, do you hear it?
The pulse does not die at the sound of it.

The heart does not crush at the weight of it.
Hands have quieted over the table top.

They are still and pleased with having nothing to do.
It is this end that they have prayed for.

Winter has shut itself off so suddenly; so has love.
Even the sun shows no mercy today.

— Louise Masino-Cotter
March 2, 1981

Eight: Proof

Over a period of several years, my obsession with what happened gradually faded like the ghost himself. It is true that I had not looked back on these experiences so thoroughly, vividly, and with such perspective until that day in the Pry House Field Hospital Museum in Sharpsburg, Maryland, when I somehow conjured up just the right mixture of curiosity and nostalgia to bring it all back.

It sent me on a two year journey to dig up the evidence, retrace the steps I had taken so many years ago, and write it all down. I was even able to find the jar and newspaper buried in the back of a closet in my parent's basement.

I washed the grime away from the jar and discarded the old trash bag the newspaper had been in, placing it into a new protective plastic cover. I set them both out on the kitchen table and looked over them as if I was being reunited with old friends. In an instant I could feel the essence of the house again. That positive buzzing energy was back and I sensed that Walter—whoever he is—was right there, and maybe had been there all along.

Later in my search, about a month after the first draft of the book was finished, I also found several ripped out pages from my old ghost hunting journal, including the following entries (now also enclosed in plastic). These are the only two excerpts I have concerning Walter's house, verbatim.

The first thing that struck me when going over these entries, that also demonstrates how my life has continued to be strangely intertwined with the house and its ghost, was that I wrote the first one on July 13, 1997—exactly ten years to the day that I would be diagnosed with cancer on Friday, July 13, 2007.

As I implied in the introduction, it also turns out that some of the events had gotten scrambled in my memory or were completely forgotten over time. There are a few new and exciting details in these entries that I then left out of the story on purpose because they, and the fact that I somehow forgot about them, add something to the overall mystery of my experiences and how my brain chose to remember them.

Therefore, the following original documents provide a slightly different but very real, chronological account of what happened.

You will also notice that I make a lot of mistakes with my eleven-year-old grammar and historical research skills. The history you have read of My Lady's Manor earlier in the book is accurate.

The old tape recorder and tapes are also long gone. But I still have all the photos of the house and the one of Walter. The Mason jar, newly polished, is sitting on my bookshelf today. These and my journal entries are the only proof I have, and may be all that's left of the house and its most infamous resident.

Enjoy.

Where is Walter?

July 13, 1997

"My Lady's Manor," built by Lord Baltimore in 1773, is not only home to almost 10,000 acres of land, but also home to a variety of ghosts. Set between Hess Road and Old York Road is the Manor Tavern, a restaurant that was once (supposedly) an inn more than 100 years ago.

Along beside it are two equally as old, equally as haunted houses—one occupied, one abandoned. The abandoned house is known to many as "Walter's House."

When the restaurant first began its business, the place was refurnished. It is unknown when the hauntings began, but when the beds removed from the inn were just thrown out, some spirits were probably aroused.

At first I was under the impression that the ghost was a man, being that its name was "Walter." I later found out that there was also a female, and possibly a poltergeist. Footsteps, movement of objects, voices, and screams are all supplemented to the many different ghost sightings.

Dad took a job there and graciously asked other employees about their experiences for me. Many people said that a ghostly human shape sits by the fire near the bar each night around 2:00 a.m. Some reported objects moving by themselves, or lost and found, and others described strange feelings and presences. Most were reluctant to go into much detail, though. Then there was the story of the man who was alone early in the morning in the Tavern when a woman dressed in old clothes came wafting through the room. As she walked by, she asked, "Where is Walter?" with little expression on her face and just disappeared. So after the incident, all the ghosts became known as "Walter."

When I heard this, I decided to do a little research myself. On September 1, 1996 at 11:30 pm, I packed my ghost-hunting material and headed off to "Walter's house." The house had been abandoned for more than 40 years probably and was musty and torn apart by reckless teenagers. The house was still sturdy and I approached carefully and positively. With one flashlight between me and my mother, I entered.

The door had been long broken apart and the broken windows allowed the faintest string of moonlight to show through. We stepped into the living room. Although the fireplace was intact, there was rubble and debris thrown everywhere, with holes in the wall in addition to that. I was left stranded in the small room as my mother took the flashlight into the kitchen. The kitchen was torn apart like everything else, with a big refrigerator right in the middle of it. The sun porch next to the room revealed a giant ivy patch.

Still in the living room, I noticed a small closet on my left. I stepped into it to see what was in it. It wasn't a closet. It was the basement stairs! I screamed.

My mother came to see what I was yelling about and we both came to the conclusion that we should get the hell out of there—fast. It seemed like slow motion as we stumbled out of the house, jumped off the porch (almost into the road), and raced to our car. I took a look behind me, and saw a tall, dark silhouette of a man either running with us, or running after us. The last though I had that night was a thought of grief. "What a fine apparition-hunter I make."

With little success for the weeks to come, I searched the house over and over, getting to know the mysterious warmth of "Walter."

Soon after that, a terrible accident occurred. A woman, driving drunk along Old York Road, somehow swerved through the bushes and right into "Walter's" yard. As she headed straight into the house, her car took a sharp curve right around it, barely missing the porch. She had been knocked out already for quite a while, but somehow, all alone in the car, she missed death. Could Walter have been a part of this? That was my first assumption.

Thinking back on that September night, I decided that going back to Walter's at night would be a good thing to try. So my parents and I ventured out on the evening of February 2, with great success.

This night had the perfect setting for ghosts—a full moon with freshly fallen snow. Although my family and I were unsuccessful in opening the attic door, we managed to explore everything else. We kept the tape recorder out and on as we searched the many rooms of the upstairs and downstairs. We left the place with a religious magazine from March (my birth month) of 1954 (my mom's birth year), a Mason jar, a newspaper from Friday, December 13, 1946, and a voice on my tape recorder. What did this mean? I don't know.

I later found out that on the recorder was the voice of a man saying, "Take that, take it, now!" in a nervous voice. This was the approximate time that we had discovered the newspaper. Was this going to be yet another ghost to add to my list?

All this inspired my "Ghost Speech" at school and my "Ghost Tour." My ghost tour consisted of my friend Graham Snodgrass and I. We toured the house and its ground and took pictures. I noticed, as I visited the place, that there was a new warmth and comfort, something I hadn't felt that September evening. Suddenly, I wasn't as frightened. Graham and I not only heard footsteps and a voice, but we managed to get the attic door open. Hearing the sound of bats, we closed it up again. We also noticed that most of the ghostly "signs" were those of a man.

I wished I could see Walter and I openly said so. To my luck, as we turned away to leave the house, there in the right attic window was "Walter" himself, looking down on us. Graham definitely saw him, but my mother was too slow to look. It was the greatest five seconds of accomplishment of my life.

I realize that there and still are so many pieces missing to the puzzle. I have taken many pictures. Faint shapes, full body shapes, strange lights, and weird objects all appear in my photographs. I am now continuing research on the house and the area.

An Entry about Walter's House

November 24, 1997

Recently I found out that Walter's House has been completely torn down. A week before that I was at the house.

I went to see the land and it looked as if nothing had ever been there. The source of my inspiration, my career, my happiness; it's all gone. I cried.

I wrote a poem to honor it. It scared me, comforted me, chased me, brought me back, and I cared about the place.

When I left the last time I had been there, I had thought of what a fantastic place it was. I never really realized what it had meant to me. Now it's gone. It's almost as if someone has died.

The house felt pain. Maybe its trapped occupants and the house itself now have peace. Their mystery is solved.

I loved that place.

About the Author

Amelia Cotter is an author and native Marylander who lives and writes in Chicago. She graduated from Hood College with a degree in German and History. She loves animals and shares her home with her dog, Oskar and snake, Atticus. Amelia's other passion is, of course, the paranormal. Her books for young adults, children, and ghost story enthusiasts of all ages include the top seller *This House: The True Story of a Girl and a Ghost*, *Maryland Ghosts: Paranormal Encounters in the Free State*, and *Breakfast with Bigfoot* (ages 3-6). Amelia also enjoys writing haiku, and her poetry has been featured in journals like *Acorn*, *The Heron's Nest*, and the *Anthology of English Language Haiku by Women*.

Amelia was Assistant Director of the Chicago Ghost Hunters Group before co-founding the Chicago Paranormal Seekers in 2010. She has been a guest speaker on programs like Darkness Radio and at paranormal conferences in and around Chicago.

You can find Amelia on Facebook and LinkedIn, or you can write to her any time at ameliamcotter@gmail.com.

About the Editor

Michelle Jacksier is an assistant vice-president and Web Managing Editor for the Federal Home Loan Bank of Chicago. Admittedly, she has more degrees in languages and literatures than is really useful for her career in Corporate Communications. A lover of the innate human ability for expressive communications and self-diagnosed grammar geek, she has written and edited numerous banking and financial publications, and is on her way to becoming a social-media maven.

Preview of *Maryland Ghosts: Paranormal Encounters in the Free State*

A chilling collection of personal paranormal encounters gathered from friends, family, and fellow paranormal investigators in some of Maryland's most legendary haunted locations, as well as private homes, public, hidden, and sometimes unexpected places.

From "The Log Cabin," Ellicott City, Howard County:

...The cabin had a long driveway that sat at a 45-degree angle and was frozen in the fall and winter, forcing my dad to park at the bottom and walk through the woods to get home. He says there was a 20-foot long bridge he had to drive over, and then he would park and have to cross some wooden planks going over a stream and navigate through the trees up to the cabin. If it was nighttime, and there was no moonlight, he'd have to feel his way home. It would be so dark, he couldn't see the cabin.

For the first two months he lived there, he had trouble sleeping because it was so quiet, and so utterly dark.

His paranormal encounter occurred a few months into living there, in the late winter of 1981, around February or March. He was alone in the cabin and in his bedroom studying for one of his classes. He didn't have the television or any music on. Everything was silent, and suddenly something just didn't feel right.

He calmly got up and went into the living room to read, but something still wasn't right. "I just had this eerie feeling suddenly," he said. "I started to look around the cabin apprehensively. I made a right to go into the kitchen after checking Tom's room. There was a front door in the living room and another door in the kitchen we never used to come in and out, with no curtains on the windows. Looking into the kitchen, and out into the dark, I *felt* it."

He could see into the bathroom from there as well, and with the bathroom door open he could see the toilet and the sink. The door was about three quarters of the way open, which means there was just enough room for someone to be standing behind it.

"I remember standing there thinking that there was *someone* behind that door. I wasn't going to walk in there and find out. I was scared. I mean *scared*. I dashed out to my car and left. I actually drove to a shopping center and sat there for a couple of hours until I thought it was safe to go back. I just sat in my car waiting..."

From "The Devil in Hagerstown," Hagerstown, Washington County:

"...I heard the chain on the door, the inside lock, begin to rattle as if someone was entering my residence. I reached for my revolver. I heard, and could almost feel, heavy footsteps advancing down my hallway, past my library, and into my bedroom.

"Before me appeared a large black, translucent form, approximately seven feet tall. My ceilings in that townhouse apartment were about nine feet tall for reference.

"I sensed that the 'form' before me was a masculine one, and it was not the first time I had ever sensed it, but was the first time I had ever seen it. Was it 'death' or 'the devil' that I had before me, after so many years?

"My heavy pistol was of no use to me at this moment.

"I greeted the 'vision' with the verbal demand to leave me and leave my home, for dying was not an option. The black form seemed to change shape as I yelled at him. He wasn't going easily and neither was I, as I had too much to live for.

"After approximately ten minutes, I saw my clock, it was 3:25am, and my 'visitor' slowly turned away from me. I could hear his heavy footsteps walking back down the hall (yet he seemed to hover when near me).

He entered my kitchen, and I could hear the chain rattle on my back door as he left. The next thing I recall was the sun coming up. I still had my pistol in hand and I rose from my bed to reconstruct, at least in my mind, what had occurred only a few hours earlier.

I had nice wooden floors and sectional rugs. The rugs had been disturbed as if someone or something had ruffled them up. A few of my books that had been on the glass coffee table seemed to have been knocked to the floor..."

CPSIA information can be obtained at www.ICGtesting.com
Printed in the USA
BVOW050743300911

272477BV00002B/33/P